INSTRUCTOR'S MANUAL

COMPUTER AND DIGITAL SYSTEM ARCHITECTURE

William D. Murray

University of Colorado at Denver

D1712158

PRENTICE HALL
Englewood Cliffs, New Jersey 07632

© 1990 by **PRENTICE-HALL, INC.**
A Division of Simon & Schuster
Englewood Cliffs, N.J. 07632

10 9 8 7 6 5 4 3 2 1

ISBN 0-13-165747-X
Printed in the United States of America

CONTENTS

PREFACE

This manual is designed to assist instructors in teaching courses using the text Computer and Digital System Architecture. In the manual I include suggestions on how to approach the course, key objectives of each chapter, solutions to many problems and discussions of others, and recommendations on using and building on the appendices. I shall appreciate any suggestions from anyone who uses the text and the manual. I shall attempt to answer any questions that readers of the manual wish to address to me at:

Professor William D. Murray
Campus Box 165
University of Colorado at Denver
1200 Larimer Street
Denver, CO 80204

bitnet: WMURRAY @ CUDENVER

I hope that there are few errors in the text or in this manual. Corrections for those I have found in the first printing of the text are listed below. If you find any others, please let me know in order that they can be removed in subsequent printings.

Errors in first printing (corrections in bold print):

p.227, Figure 6-22: exchange B_1 and A_1, B_0 and A_0.

p.249, Problem 6-7, line 5: **32**-bit...

p.294, Figure 7-32, line 2: {**16** banks...

p.361, line 19: $x_i - (j-1)$

p.362, Figure 9-10: $x_i - (j-1)$

p.384, Problem 9-2, line 5: with $m = u = 100$.

OVERVIEW

The text contains material I have used in teaching a course,
Advanced Computer Architecture, for graduate students in
Electrical Engineering and Computer Science. In teaching the
course a number of times over the years I have used different
balances between lecture and discussion. I have felt most
satisfied with the results when I have been able to get the
students involved in reporting on and arguing about different
computer organizations. Discussion can be held on all levels of
computer architecture, from the top system level all the way down
to the integrated-circuit level. (Of course, the level and the
nature of detail will vary according to the backgrounds of the
students.)

As a result, I encourage you to ask the students to contribute to
the learning process. They should investigate real computers by
reading technical journals, pouring over manufacturers' manuals,
and discussing computer characteristics with computer services
personnel and with users. While those students who do not have
strong experience with computers initially are reluctant to
express their opinions, I have found that they become active
participants after a few sessions, particularly if the instructor
shows an interest in hearing their ideas. In fact, some of these
students appear to have gained the most from the course. Mature
students who are working with computers get involved very
quickly, particularly when they hear claims about the benefits of
some computer with which they are not familiar

With this "get involved" approach, by the end of the course
students can be expected to be able to perform a computer design at
the architecture level, or to evaluate different vendor offerings
for satisfying a computer need. A significant number of the
students who have taken the course have quickly become active
members of computer or digital system design and evaluation
teams.

You will note a design-oriented approach in the text. After
outlining a design methodology and defining descriptive tools, I
have presented alternative approaches at the system and the
subsystem levels of computer architecture. There is emphasis on
"these are the ways you might", rather than "this is how you
should". It is important that the instructor reinforce this
approach by identifying the advantages of different architectures
and different example computers. (This can be difficult if you,
like I, were raised in a particular school of computer design.)
The fact that there are a number of successful computer
manufacturers with different approaches to computer architecture
helps to demonstrate that there is "more than one way to do it".

The amount and the depth of coverage of the material in the text
will depend on the background of the students. If they have an
understanding of at least one particular computer, at least to
the level of assembly-language programming, and of programming
languages and operating systems, all of the text can be covered
in a semester. Graduate students who are computer professionals
are able to cover the whole text in significant depth. On the
other hand, if the background of the students, the interests of
the instructor, or the objectives of the course call for

different coverage, it is easy to de-emphasize or to eliminate some of the material. A successful course can be conducted using chapters 1 through 7 and 10, or all chapters can be covered with more detailed investigation devoted to chapters 2, 3, 4, and 5. It is more important to get students to actively participate in what is covered than it is to cover everything.

As you review the problems I have included at the end of Chapters 2 through 9 you will find that most are design-oriented and open-ended. This is in keeping with the objectives I have laid out. In this manual I have included discussions and suggestions about what to look for from the students, as well as my answers to some of the problems. (Usually there are other correct answers.) A specific answer is less important than the process of arriving at an answer. The most interesting design problems are those that have no answer or multiple correct answers.

I encourage you to assign one or two projects to be conducted throughout the course. Starting with Chapter 1, I have carried two projects through the text, specifying the parts that should be accomplished on the subjects of each chapter. The first is a project to investigate a computer system and the second is a computer system design. Either (or both) can be a very useful experience for students. Included also are "miniprojects" on the topics of chapters 2 through 9. These can be particularly useful if you do not find sufficient time for a comprehensive project, or they can augment the latter.

You will note that there are two appendices to the text. A formal definition of the descriptive languages that are used throughout the book is covered in Appendix A. In Appendix B you will find programming-level descriptions of seven contemporary computer architectures. These are IBM System/370, DEC VAX, Motorola M68000, National Semiconductor NS32000, Intel 80386, MIPS RISC, and Sun SPARC. I suggest that you review the appendices, perhaps after reading Chapters 1 and 2, to determine how you might best use the material contained in them. The content of the appendices and their uses are summarized at the end of this Manual.

The list of references is fairly comprehensive and should lead students to any degree of depth desired on specific topics. I have attempted to add references at the latest possible date, considering production schedules. You will find more recent papers on many subjects. I encourage you to have your students dig into the current literature to identify new ideas and the reincarnations of older ones.

There are several approaches to examinations. I prefer to limit these to a midterm and a final exam, placing grading emphasis on the projects. The problems at the end of each chapter are representative of questions that a colleague, Harry F. Jordan of the University of Colorado at Boulder, and I have used in examinations. Examination questions can require descriptive answers or quantitative responses. I suggest that you use the type of exam that best matches your course objectives.

Chapter 1 INTRODUCTION

This chapter sets the tone for the course. I include an outline of what is covered in the text, showing that we will develop a design methodology and will investigate the alternatives that are available for design at the various architecture levels.

The section on history of computers is included to demonstrate that computer architecture is a mature discipline and to show that today's computer architectures are the result of an evolutionary process. We have learned from architectures of the past, and the successful architectures that have lasted have themselves evolved through advances in technology.

It is important to introduce early the fact that there is a variety of computer organizations. The variations exist at the system level and at subsystem levels. The alternatives in this chapter are included to establish that differences exist, not to be the subject of detailed study themselves.

If we are to describe architectures precisely, it is desirable that we have descriptive mechanisms to permit precise and concise specification of those architectures. Description languages for computer architecture, the Processor-Memory-Switch (PMS) and the Instruction-Set Processor (ISP) languages, are introduced in this chapter. Here, again, the objective is to introduce the concepts, and more detailed discussion follows in later chapters.

Even at this introductory stage it is not too early to have students address the question of how they would (individually or in groups) design a computer to meet some specific requirements. It is useful to have them investigate the differences between or among example architectures. A quick investigation as a homework assignment will serve to get them started on their term projects. The starting point for project A should be a determination of where they should go to get the detailed information needed for a complete description of a computer architecture.

For students who are employed with firms that have computer centers they might visit those centers to find out whether they can gain access to the computer user manuals that describe the architectures. These usually have titles like "Hardware Description Manual" and "Programmer's Reference Manual". The former describe the system configurations that are possible (PMS level) and the latter describe the computer that is seen by the programmer (ISP). Similar information should be available in college and university computer centers. Usually the sales offices of computer manufacturers will provide students with documentation, if they are not descended on by large numbers of students at one time. I have found it useful to collect manuals on various computers to be used by students who have difficulty finding the information on their own.

If students are undertaking the design project (B), they should start by defining the applications for which the computer will be used. They can think of the applications of the firm that employs them, of those of the school's computers, or they might develop their own ideas of how they would like a computer to be used.

Chapter 2 DESIGN METHODOLOGY AND DESCRIPTIVE TOOLS

If we are going to design something we need an objective for the design, and we need to be able to determine when we have met the objective. This chapter establishes a design methodology that starts with the requirements for which a computer will be designed. It is important that students appreciate that design can start only after the users' requirements are clear. Those students who have taken a course in software engineering or in system analysis and design will be familiar with this top-down approach, but they might not appreciate that the approach is as useful in hardware development as in software design.

We are introduced to the place of the computer architect in an organization. The top-down design methodology that moves in an orderly way from system requirements to the final design is covered. We are encouraged to work from the overall system to the details. You might have examples of designs that were unsuccessful because they did not follow this orderly approach. They can demonstrate more easily than abstract descriptions the benefits of the top-down methodology.

This chapter includes an informal definition of languages for computer description. The definitions are sufficiently detailed that students can use and read PMS, ISP, and Register Transfer Languages. A formal definition of PMS and ISP is included in Appendix A. The existence of the appendix should be introduced at this point. It is useful as a reference, no matter what level of detail you choose to use in the course.

Just as we wish to have students think of designs that respond to requirements, we should also raise their concern about economic issues. They should understand that each commercially successful computer architecture has competitive performance at competitive cost, as well as being technically interesting. It can be useful to introduce some "bad examples" here to get the point across. There is nothing like the example of a failure to demonstrate the characteristics of a success.

Problems 2-1 through 2-5 and 2-11 encourage thinking about the issues of computer architecture and about the design methodology. I have used questions like this to get the students investigating and discussing. I look for thought and reason in their answers, rather than for correctness.

After students have completed Problem 2-6, 2-8, or 2-9 you might have them read others' descriptions of these machines. The von Neumann papers [BurkA46] and the Intel 8086 Manual [Intel79] are useful here. I have found that students benefit from comparisons and discussions of their individual interpretations.

As the students start on their projects it is beneficial to establish intermediate milestones in their schedules. I suggest that you require progress reports covering the material of each chapter, to be submitted a week after the chapter has been discussed. The downside of this is that you must review and return the reports quickly in order that you not retard their progress toward project completion.

4

Chapter 3 SYSTEM STRUCTURE (THE PMS LEVEL)

In this chapter we review the various ways that a computer system can be configured. The emphasis is on system organization. It is too easy for us all to focus on the processor rather than the system organization when comparing computers. We are more used to looking at the assembly language level of the computer than the broader level.

In order to get the students thinking in terms of the systems level we might suggest that we are starting a new computer company and we wish to compete with the "big guys". How can we introduce a family of computers with a significant performance range? How can we offer an organization that is different and has advantages over what now exists? How do we satisfy a need--or fill a niche? Can we offer improved performance, more flexibility of configuration, increased reliability, a specialization?

Interesting system issues include how the parts are connected and how they communicate. Since there are so many satisfactory ways to connect computer modules, and since no one interconnection scheme is best, we need to look at performance and cost issues to place some measures on the alternatives.

Once we have seen the various system organizations we can focus on the subsystems, the parts. This chapter introduces the major subsystems, but only to the level of detail needed to understand the system alternatives. The individual subsystems are covered in detail in later chapters. A discussion of the problems included in this chapter will serve to outline the system issues that should be emphasized.

Problem 3-1. Students are asked to "design" a system that uses existing computer (VAX) modules. The PMS diagram below shows how Digital did it with the asymetric attached processor system VAX-11/782. Both the primary processor and the attached processor are VAX-11/780s. Multiple VAX computers with local memory units also can share a multiport memory or can be connected through the DR-32 Device Interconnect. In both cases the result is a multicomputer system. Later VAX models included symmetric multiprocessor versions, such as the VAX 8800, a multiprocessor VAX 8700 (Fig. 3-8). It is useful to compare and discuss students' and Digital's approaches.

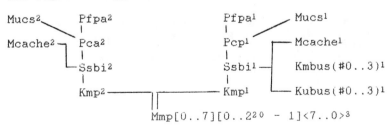

1. "VAX-11/780_Primary_Processor" {see text Fig. 3-3 for detail}
2. "VAX-11/780_Attached_Processor" {has no independent I/O}
3. Mmp\"Multiport_Memory" {shared by Pcp and Pca}

Problems 3-2 and 3-3. There is a tendency to oversimplify here.
Get the students to think of the issues: communications capacity,
switch design, subsystem control. These problems can lead to
interesting class discussion.

Problem 3-4. The issues include recovery of message sequence,
erroneous packet retransmission, missing packets, timing, what
the sender does before the message is received.

Problem 3-5 (a). This is a (16000, 16000, 8000) switch. It looks
like a crossbar that is symmetric about the diagonal. Since a
single connection is bidirectional it can be built from 8000
(15999, 1, 1) tree switches, with complexity of 128×10^6.
    (b), (c). The required (16000, 16000, 512) switch can be
implemented with 512 (16000, 16000, 1) tree/inverted-tree
switches, with a complexity of $16000 \times 2 \times 512 = 16 \times 10^6$.

Problem 3-6. The (2000, 2000, 1000) party-line switch requires
2000 (1999, 1, 1) trees. Each party-line group is on a bus. The
complexity is $8 \times 2000 \times 2000 = 32 \times 10^6$. The number of
simultaneous calls can be reduced as in Problem 3-5 (b).

Problem 3-7. Students will find many ways to respond to these
requirements. Look for the reasons behind their "designs". This
system has two "producer" computers feeding information to, and
four "consumer" computers taking information from, the computer
being designed. The total average rate of information transferred
is about 200,000 bytes/s. This will be doubled if we include
transfers to and from secondary memory of our computer. To allow
for surges of produced and consumed data the input/output system
should have a "bandwidth" of at least two Mbytes/s. Central
processor performance of about two million operations per second
probably allows for the processing needed to coordinate producer
and consumer processes. A 16-bit processor probably is adequate.
Modular primary memory, and multiple disk files with controllers
and a switch that allows concurrent activity will provide the
transfer rates needed. The system switch (multiple trees?) should
allow simultaneous transfers of information between the object
computer and at least two of the producers/consumers.

Problems 3-8 and 3-9. There a several ways that each of these
systems can be configured. Students might fill in some "blanks"
by providing missing data. These make for good class discussion.

Problem 3-10 (a). The failure probability is the sum of failure
probabilities of both processors (0.02^2) plus 2, 3, or all 4
memory modules $(0.005^2 + 0.005^3 + 0.005^4)$ plus 2 or all 3 Pio
$(0.01^2 + 0.01^3)$. The result to 2 significant digits is 5×10^{-4}.
    (b). $(2 \times 0.02 + 4 \times 0.005 + 3 \times 0.01) = 9 \times 10^{-2}$.

Problems 3-11 through 3-14 have no "right" answers. They form a
basis for good class discussion.

Projects A and B. This is the system design or description step.

Project 3-C is a mini-project to compare systems approaches. You
should determine if the approaches taken appear reasonable and if
the solutions reflect thinking about cost and performance.

Chapter 4 THE 'MEMORY HIERARCHY

The starting point in this chapter is an understanding that the reason we need more than one level of memory is the relative cost of memory devices at different performance levels. If we build a computer only with the lowest cost memory it will be too slow, whereas if we use the highest performance devices it will be too expensive. You might want to discuss the hypothesis that, "We can use as much memory as we want because it is so cheap."

The degree of detail that you go into on the devices will depend on the backgrounds of students. Even for those who are not electrical engineers (maybe mostly for them) it is important that they understand why different memory types have different costs. I find that "non-techie" students understand transistor counts and the basic principles of memory with moving magnetic media.

With all the different technologies available (and the continued search for other technologies) it is most important that students face the tradeoffs that must be considered. The objective in memory design is optimization of performance/cost when a system is used with different process mixes. The examples of successful systems will show that different approaches can be satisfactory.

Problem 4-1 (a). Starting with unity cost in 1970 I find that in 10 years the cost is reduced to 4×10^{-2}. Therefore, in 30 years (2000) the cost will be 64×10^{-6} or about 10^{-4} cents/bit.
   (b). Similarly, unity cycle time in 1968 and 1.2×10^{-1} in 1978 extends to a cycle time of 8×10^{-4} microseconds in 2000.
   I use projections of this type in Chapter 10.

Problem 4-2. Data in the chapter indicates if DRAM Mp unit cost is unity, then SRAM Mp unit cost is 6 to 8 (say 7) and SRAM Mcache unit cost is 12 to 16 (say 14). Cost of a is $4 \times 1.05 \times 10^6 + 14 \times 16 \times 1.02 \times 10^3 = 4.4 \times 10^6$. Smaller b costs $7 \times 2 \times 1.05 \times 10^6 = 15 \times 10^6$. Mp a is almost as fast as b. The smaller size of b could lead to more Ms transfers, affecting system performance.

Problem 4-3. Cost differences between the two memory approaches: Memory a is a little more expensive, since each module requires a power supply and addressing circuitry. The bus for b is more costly if transfers are to be made as 128-bit parallel quadwords. If the quadwords are separated into individual 32-bit words, transferred in sequence, and reassembled, then more timing and control circuits are required.
   On performance: For block transfers, if bus a can transfer at 4 times the rate of b the block transfer times will be the same. Otherwise a will be slower. For random access to individual words in memory, performance will be proportional to bus cycle time. In this case there is wasted bus capacity in b.
   The reliability of a will be better, since the memory can be reconfigured (by reloading from Ms) in event of a module failure. The failure probability of a module of a is 1/4 that of b. If the system can perform satisfactorily when only three modules are in service the unreliability of a is 1/16 that of b since two modules must fail for system failure.

Problem 4-4. My programs (with times in parentheses) are:

Single accumulator, Ac:			Registers R0, R1, R2, R3:			
ClrAdd	A	(100)	Load	R0	A	(100)
Add	B	(100)	Load	R1	B	(100)
Store	Temp1	(100)	Add	R1	R0	(20)
ClrAdd	C	(100)	Load	R2	C	(100)
Sub	D	(100)	Load	R3	D	(100)
Mult	Temp1	(100)	Sub	R3	R2	(20)
Store	E	(100)	Mul	R2	R0	(20)
ClrAdd	A	(100)	Store	R0	E	(100)
Sub	B	(100)	Load	R2	A	(100)
Store	Temp1	(100)	Sub	R1	R2	(20)
ClrAdd	C	(100)	Load	R1	C	(100)
Add	D	(100)	Add	R3	R1	(20)
Mult	Temp1	(100)	Mul	R2	R1	(20)
Store	F	(100)	Store	R1	F	(100)
Add	E	(100)	Copy	R0	R2	(20)
Store	A	(100)	Add	R2	R0	(20)
ClrAdd	E	(100)	Store	R0	A	(100)
Sub	F	(100)	Sub	R1	R2	(20)
Store	B	(100)	Store	R2	B	(100)
Total time =		(1900)	Total time =			(1180)

Problem 4-5. This problem is designed to get readers thinking
about some of the details of cache/primary memory interaction.
The "signaling" must be done in time to not itself cause a
slowdown of memory operation. Bus transfer times will affect the
three cache approaches differently. When the cache is at the
processors (Fig. 3-23(a)) communication with Mp is needed only
after a cache miss, and (with read operations) a cache reference
that hits will not slow the other Pc. After cache writes cache
coordination is required. With cache at Mp (Fig. 3-23(b)) the two
clock times for transfer of address and receipt of data must be
added to cache and Mp read times. In this case Mp can start a
read cycle as its cache is being checked and the read can be
aborted if there is a hit. The approach with a separate cache
(Fig. 3-23(c)) has advantages and disadvantages of each of the
other two.

Problem 4-6. Transferring a block of data from Ms appears as:

```
a- time 0        8       16
    Ms  |access| xfer | ---------- |access| xfer |--
    Pc  -proc.-> xfer <----processing----> xfer <----


b- time 0          12          24      32
    Ms    |   access   |   xfer    |---------|   access   |   xfer    |--
  buffer                           | xfer |
    Pc    ----processing--------> xfer <-------processing------->
```

If Ms references can be initiated well before the block is needed
there is no difference in the performances of the two Ms designs
when there is 50 ms between references. At 25 ms the interblock
time is close to the (access + transfer) time of b. The minimum
interblock transfer time of a is 16 ms and b's is 24 ms. Transfer
times of the buffer and of each Ms is proportional to block size,
and processor transfer times will be the same for both designs.

Problem 4-7 (a). At any level i the independent probability of a hit p_i = H. The probability of a miss q_i = 1 - H. The probability that a hit occurs by any level is P_i. The probability that a hit has not occurred is Q_i = 1 - P_i. P_i = $p_i * Q_{i-1}$ = H * Q_{i-1}; P_0 = $p_0 * 1$ = H; P_1 = H (1 - H); P_i = H $(1 - H)^i$.

(b). The expected access time is the sum through all levels of individual access times multiplied by individual P_i. This is T_a = t_{a0} (H + H(1 - H)k + ... + H$(1 - H)^i k^i$), (1 = 0,1,2...), which converges to H/(1-k(1-H)) if k(1-H) < 1.

(c). If the miss ratio is inversely proportional to access time, q_i = $q_0 k^{-1}$. Let q_0 = 1 - H = Q_0. Q_1 = $q_0 * q_0/k$. Q_2 = $q_0 * q_0/k * q_0/k^2$. In general Q_i = q_0^{i+1} / $k^{SUM\ j}$, (j = 1,2...i). Again P_i = $p_i * Q_{i-1}$ or P_i = $(1 - q_0/k^i)(q_0^i/k^{SUM\ j})$, (j = 1,2...i-1). The expected access time T_a = SUM ($t_{aj} * P_j$) = t_{a0}(SUM ($k^j * q_0^j (1-q_0/k^j)/k^{(j*j-j)/2}$) = , (j = 0,1...). This converges for all values of k.

Problem 4-8. With larger physical (n words) than virtual (m words) memory (as in the XDS940) there is a page frame entry in the page table for every virtual page. Therefore memory mapping simply entails using the page value of m bits as a direct address into a 2^m-word table of n-bit words to get the physical block (frame) address.

Problem 4-9. In both cases we start with the virtual address. Each ISP description should include the address translation from page or segment to block or base address and the addition of the offset. There should be checks for presence in physical memory and transfer from Ms if the block or segment is not present. A range check might be included to determine if the address is out of bounds with the approach of Fig. 4-19.

Problem 4-10. The desired bit sequence is 1101 0110, and (with odd parity) p = 0, c_1 = 0, c_2 = 0, c_3 = 0, c_4 = 0. The full word transmitted (with parity and redundant bits is 0 0010 1010 0110. In case (a) the word received is 0 0010 1010 0010. There is a parity error, showing an odd number of errors. Multiplying the syndrome of Fig. 4-23 by the received vector without the parity bit yields (modulo 2 values) the bit sequence 1010 = 10d. There is an error in the 10th bit location (underlined above), and the correct value is 0010 1010 0110, (with c_i removed 1101 0110). In (b) 0 0010 1010 1010 is received. Parity is correct and there is an even number of errors (0,2,4...). The syndrome is multiplied by the vector 0010 1010 1010 to yield 0011 = 3. There is at least one error. With the correct parity we can only deduce that there are 2 errors. (In general we cannot find 4, 6, 8... errors.)

Project 4-C. You should find interesting different memory system designs. They should be checked for consistency among sizes and speeds of memories at each level, and for the switches.

Chapter 5 THE INSTRUCTION-SET PROCESSOR

This chapter covers the computer that is seen by the machine- or assembly-language programmer. Students should be familiar with at least one computer to this level of detail, but they probably do not realize that there are many different successful ISPs. It is important to consider why there should be these differences and to question any feelings that there is a "best" ISP. I have found it useful to have students address the subject by having them determine the ISPs they would design for their applications.

The chapter reviews programming languages and operating systems to establish a framework for ISP design. Even if students have strong backgrounds in these topics, usually they have not considered the effects on and the effects of computer ISPs. Thus Sections 5.2 and 5.3 form more than a review.

Section 5.4 on Processor State describes the organizations and uses of registers in processors. The connection of register issues to operating system and language issues is covered in Section 5.5. The use of registers to hold data and instructions of different formats is discussed in Sections 5.6 and 5.7.

Throughout the chapter examples of actual computers are included to demonstrate that the concepts and issues are real. The use of a variety of commercially successful computer examples shows that there is no "best" ISP organization. You might find it useful to use some of the detailed examples of ISPs in Appendix B to demonstrate both obvious and subtle differences among computers that students are familiar with.

The subject of ISPs is not complete without addressing issues of control, covered in Chapter 6. I suggest that you review the latter yourself before lecturing on Chapter 5.

Problem 5-1.

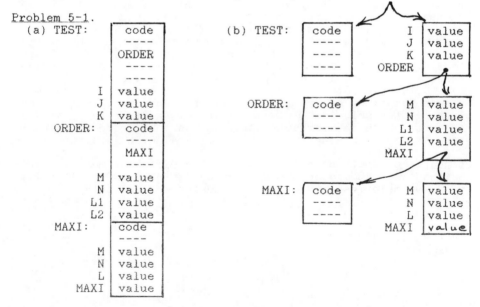

Problem 5-2 (a). Using the approach with indirect designators at the destination (Fig. 5-22(c)), the resource semaphore will contain values (indirect bit = 0) in Identification, Creator, and Quantity words; the address (indirect bit = 1) of the start of the Resource Waiting List; and the address (indirect bit = 1) of the first word of the Allocator Code. The heading of the Resource Waiting List will contain four pointers (addresses, with indirect bit = 1) to the first words of the Insert Code, the Remove Code, the Process Descriptor at the Head of the Waiting List, and the Process Descriptor at the Tail of the Waiting List. Each Process Descriptor would contain values (indirect = 0) followed by a pointer (indirect = 1) to the first word of the next Process Descriptor. All words of the codes will have indirect = 0.

(b). A register B[base] contains the base address of the memory segment. The offset to the desired argument is in ARG of the instruction. The size of the segment is contained in a register R[range]. Physical addressing proceeds (in ISP) as:
    ARG LE R[range] -> argument <- Mp[R[base] + ARG].

Problem 5-3 (a, b). For the one- and two-address computers:
    Instructions (ARG, SOURCE, and DESTIN are memory locations):

```
            CLRADD ARG              ADD SOURCE DESTIN
            STORE ARG               SUB SOURCE DESTIN
            ADD ARG                 MUL SOURCE DESTIN
            SUB ARG                 DIV SOURCE DESTIN
            MUL ARG                 COPY SOURCE DESTIN
            DIV ARG
    Programs:
            CLRADD Mp[a]            COPY Mp[a] Mp[tm1]
            SUB Mp[d]               SUB Mp[d] Mp[tm1]
            STORE Mp[temp]          COPY Mp[b] Mp[tm2]
            CLRAD Mp[b]             ADD Mp[c] Mp[tm2]
            ADD Mp[c]               MUL Mp[a] Mp[tm2]
            MUL Mp[a]               DIV Mp[tm2] Mp[tm1]
            DIV Mp[temp]            STORE Mp[tm1] Mp[f]
            ADD Mp[e]
            STORE Mp[f]
```

To show translation directly on a stack machine (Fig.5-9) I shall use a computer different from that described in Problem 5-4. A code bit distinguishes an operator from an argument. Fifteen-bit arguments (addresses or literals) precede the operators LOAD, and PUSH (for literals). Arithmetic operators use the top two stack registers for arguments and return the result to the (new) top of the stack. POP is available to clear the top. The program is:

```
            address f              address a
            PUSH                   LOAD
            address a              address d
            LOAD                   LOAD
            address b              SUB
            LOAD                   DIV
            address c              address e
            LOAD                   LOAD
            ADD                    ADD
            MUL                    STORE
```

(c). The program in the one-address machine uses 27 bytes, for two-address it is 35 bytes, in the stack machine 27 bytes.

11

Problem 5-4.

	Computer A (R - R)	Computer B (stack)
(a). Programs	LOAD GR[1] Mp[b]	PUSH Mp[a]
	LOAD GR[2] Mp[d]	PUSH Mp[b]
	SUB GR[2] GR[1] GR[2]	ADD
	LOAD GR[3] Mp[a]	PUSH Mp[c]
	MUL GR[2] GR[3] GR[2]	DIV
	ADD GR[1] GR[1] GR[3]	PUSH Mp[a]
	LOAD GR[4] Mp[c]	PUSH Mp[b]
	DIV GR[1] GR[1] GR[4]	PUSH Mp[d]
	ADD GR[1] GR[1] GR[2]	SUB
	SUB GR[4] GR[4] GR[3]	MUL
	LOAD GR[3] Mp[e]	ADD
	DIV GR[3] GR[3] GR[4]	PUSH Mp[e]
	SUB GR[1] GR[1] GR[3]	PUSH Mp[c]
	{Note that the first	PUSH Mp[a]
	register is the target	SUB
	for the result.}	DIV
		SUB

(b).   36 bytes   44 bytes

Note the sensitivity to my assumption about bytes/instruction. If B uses 3 bytes for PUSH/POP its memory requirement is 35 bytes.

(c).   4 registers

(d). depth = 4, contents = (top) Mp[d] Mp[b] Mp[a] (a + b)/c

Problem 5-5. Register assignments. R[0,1]: top and next of stack, R[2,3]: working registers, R[4]: stack pointer (to 3rd value in stack), R[5]: stack limit in Mp, R[6]: Mp[x] address, environment boundary, R[7]: bottom of stack. The procedure requires locations in the stack in Mp for: Mp[x]: pointer to parent environment marker, Mp[x+1]: pointer to caller's environment marker, Mp[x+2]: return address, Mp[x+3]: parameter P, Mp[x+4]; parameter Q, Mp[x+5]: local A, R[1] (next of stack): local B, R[0] (top of stack): local C. Instructions for building the environment are:

```
MACRO PUSH {push top down 1 level}
        LOAD  R[3] ADDR(r)   {error routine location}
        JGE   R[4] R[5] R[3] {insufficient space}
        ADD   R[4] #1   R[4] {increment pointer}
        STORE R[1] M[R[4]]   {next into memory}
END     MOVE  R[0] R[1]      {top into next}
        CALL MACRO PUSH
        MOVE  R[6] R[0]      {old marker to stack}
        CALL MACRO PUSH
        LOAD  R[0] ADDR(p)   {parent address to stack}
        MOVE  R[4] R[6]      {location x updated}
        CALL MACRO PUSH
        LOAD  R[0] PC        {return address to stack}
        CALL MACRO PUSH
        LOAD  R[0] ADDR(c)   {caller's address to stack}
        CALL MACRO PUSH
        MOVE  R[0] lit(P)    {parameter P to stack}
        CALL MACRO PUSH
        MOVE  R[0] lit(Q)    {parameter Q to stack}
        CALL MACRO PUSH
        MOVE  R[0] lit(A)    {local A to stack}
        CALL MACRO PUSH
        MOVE  R[0] lit(B)    {local B to stack}
        CALL MACRO PUSH
        MOVE  R[0] lit(C)    {local C to stack}
```

Problem 5-6. In Pc we have the active context, held in the
General Registers and the Processor Registers shown in Fig. 5-16.
Mp contains the Process Control Blocks for the system and user
contexts, which are referred to by an operating system table:

SYS	PCB[0..23]	U1	PCB[0..23]	U2	PCB[0..23]	U3	PCB[0..23]
0	KSP	0	KSP	0	KSP	0	KSP
1	ESP	1	ESP	1	ESP	1	ESP
2	SSP	2	SSP	2	SSP	2	SSP
3	USP*	3	USP	3	USP	3	USP
4	GR[0]	4	GR[0]	4	GR[0]	4	GR[0]
	---		---		---		---
18	GR[15]	18	GR[15]	18	GR[15]	18	GR[15]
19	PSL	19	PSL	19	PSL	19	PSL
20	P0BR	20	P0BR	20	P0BR	20	P0BR
21	P0LR	21	P0LR	21	P0LR	21	P0LR
22	P1BR	22	P1BR	22	P1BR	22	P1BR
23	P1LR	23	P1LR	23	P1LR	23	P1LR

* points to stack of user contexts
    Note-All PCB registers except GR[..] and PSL contain
    addresses of memory locations where the values are held.

Problems 5-7 and 5-8. These are problems that lead to different
approaches by students. The answers to 5-7 should completely
describe in ISP the operations defined in words in the problem
statement. The example a student selects to demonstrate the
differences between the processors in Problem 5-8 will
demonstrate the degree of understanding of the differences.

Problem 5-9.

	Processor X	Processor Y	Processor Z
(a). Clock times are determined for each processor:			
Operation			
24 bits	2	2	2
48 bits	3	3	2
72 bits	5	3	3
96 bits	5	4	3
(b). Average times from the distributions of operations:			
Standard mix	2.30	2.21	2.05
Scientific mix	2.90	2.55	2.20
(c). Percentage of data space (mantissa and exponent) used:			
Standard mix	100	76	69
Scientific mix	100	80	79

(d). The reasons can be interesting.

Problem 5-10. My instruction formats are:
 First Computer-
  no argument   op<11..0>, {12 bits}
  reg. to reg.   op<10..0>, mode, reg[0..2]<3..0>, {24 bits}
  reg. / mem.   op<10..0>, mode, reg<3..0>, addr<19..0>, {36 bits}
 Second Computer- (reg = 0h means register not used)
  no argument   op<7..0>, {8 bits}
  reg. to reg.   op<7..0>, reg[0,1]<3..0>, {16 bits}
  reg. / mem.   op<7..0>, 0h, op_ext<2..0>, mode, reg[0,1]<3..0>,
                      addr[0..2][1..3]<7..0>, {16 to 96 bits}

Problem 5-11. The Intel 8086 Manual [Intel79] can be useful for
comparison with students' descriptions.

Problems 5-12 and 5-13. These "design problems" make for good discussion.

Problem 5-14. By using the first location as an instruction (CC = 0) and interpreting each instruction in sequence, we find that locations 0 through 3 contain instructions and 4 through 6 contain data. Note that an instruction's 20-bit (5-digit hex) field is truncated to 18 bits, a 3-digit hex address and a 6-bit operation. The conversion to decimal is simple, but tedious. Execution of the program requires that the ISP of Fig. 2-7 be followed precisely. The program in assembly language is:

word	program		meaning
0-left	CLA	4	Ac <- .00400h
0-right	SUB	5	Ac <- .00400h - .003A0 {= .00060h}
1-left	JCL	2	if Ac GE 0 (CC = 2, right instruction)
1-right	CLA	2	Ac <- .00400h
2-left	JML	3	jump, CC = 3, left instruction
2-right	CLA	5	Ac <- .003A0h
3-left	STO	6	Mp[006h] <- Ac
3-right	HLT		halt

The result (since the jump of 1-left is executed) is that memory location 6 contains .003A0h.

Project 5-A. Interpreting manuals to find the details of how a computer really works is a significant task. Too often students will make oversimplified assumptions, rather than taking time to find the detail.

Project 5-B. It is interesting to study the students' ISPs. Some will throw in every feature mentioned in the chapter, under the assumption that if it is discussed it must be good.

Project 5-C. You might wish to select the examples to be compared. System/370 vs. VAX, the microprocessors, 80386 vs RISC, or MIPS vs SPARC are four possibilities.

Chapter 6 PROCESSOR IMPLEMENTATION AND CONTROL

In this chapter readers focus on the differences between the
processor seen by the user, and represented by its ISP, and the
implementation of that processor. The latter is the processor
seen by the computer engineer or by the microcode designer.

Some students (particularly those who have studied control
systems) will be familiar with the ideas of state machines and
state variables. To others the ideas will be new, but should be
easy to grasp. A processor controller is a finite-state machine.
This machine can be implemented with hard-wired control using
random logic or a programmed logic array (PLA), or with software
and a microprogram or a nanoprogram.

You are faced with the question of how much detail you should
delve into in this chapter. If your students are electrical or
computer engineers it is possible to go well beyond the material
covered in the text, including detailed logic design of the
examples. Many of the readings suggested in Section 6.10 will be
worth assigning to the class. For computer science students the
material in the text should be sufficient (and is necessary, if
they are to understand how processors really work).

A major learning objective for engineering students is to
understand the applications on the technologies they are so
familiar with. Computer scientists should obtain an understanding
of the implementing technology.

The machine (Fig. 6-4) that I use as the running example is
complex enough to be representative of real computers, but simple
enough that its controls can be understood. You might wish to
make more extensive use of real processors (perhaps those whose
ISPs are in Appendix B) to demonstrate the applicability of the
concepts introduced.

The RISC/CISC argument is good for classroom discussion. While
students might argue for one or the other, I feel that the right
balance between RISC and CISC principles is the real issue. The
paper by Wirth referred to in Fig. 6-31 makes for interesting
reading along those lines.

Only one section of the book addresses ALU design. If you find
this too light a treatment because students are not familiar with
the subject, you might wish to refer to books used for
predecessor logic and computer design courses; these show much
more detail on these topics. The same books are useful as
references on details of computer control.

Two sections of the chapter address issues of computer
performance, covering some concepts and ideas, and a number of
examples. I hope that these will stimulate interest in further
investigation of computer performance by readers.

Problem 6-1. This problem appears to be simple, but deduction
about the VAX processors is required. You will get a variety of
answers. The VAX-11/780 PMS diagram (Fig. 3-3) is useful to see
what the processor is connected to. From that diagram we know
that the synchronous backplane interconnect transfers data among

15

the processor, the memory, and the I/O controllers. Figure 6-32 shows that the SBI control and the memory control are both connected to the SBI.

The processor itself can be defined with a PMS diagram. In addition to the function units (the data path includes the ALU) identified in Fig. 6-32, the general registers (Fig. 5-8) and those internal data bus registers (IDBR, Fig. 6-3) that are actually represented in a model (the architectural processor registers, APRs) must be included. Both can be added to Fig. 6-32. The internal data bus is the vehicle for moving data around the processor and the general registers and APRs are connected to it. They are controlled by the microsequencer and are destinations for the CS bus. Memory data is transferred from and to these register banks and they are both sources and destinations for the MD bus.

With these additions Fig. 6-32 is similar to a PMS diagram for the processor. We can add the width of the buses to the headings of the figure. This data is available in the VAX Hardware manual and will not be identified by most students. It shows: ID (Sid), 39 lines; V (Sv), 11 lines; PA (Spa), 28 lines; SBI (Ssbi), 32 lines; CS (Scs), 99 lines; MD (Smd), 40 lines. The manual also shows that there are 45 APRs (most shown in Fig. 6-3) in the VAX-11/780. The rest of the IDBRs are assigned memory locations.

A simpler processor is represented by the VAX-11/730. It has a simpler bus structure and fewer (29) APRs. The following is a chart similar to the augmented Fig. 6-32 for the VAX-11/780.

Buses(see definition below):	MC	IB	MA	FP	IO
Function Units:					
Memory (and UNIBUS) Controller	B		B		B
Data Path (with ALU)	B	S		B	B
Floating-point Accelerator	B	D		B	
Writeable Control Store	B				B
General Registers	B			B	B
APRs (29)	B			B	B

Bus definitions:
  MC, Memory Control, 32 lines.
  IB, Instruction Bus, 8 lines.
  MA, Memory Array (to Mp), 54 lines.
  FP, Floating-point Accelerator Port, 32 lines.
  IO, Input/Output (to UNIBUS), 56 lines.

Problem 6-2. (Students might wish to refer to the books used in logic or computer design courses for help with this and the next problem.) I assume that the instruction set includes logical, add/subtract, shift, data transfer and control instructions. The control signals are: for the ALU, s_0, s_1, s_2, and Co of Fig. 6-22; for the shifter, 2 bits for left, right, transfer, or inhibit, 1 bit for circular shift, 1 bit for logical or arithmetic shift; SA, SB, and DR use 3-bit address controls; Mask and Run flip-flops each need a control bit.

Problem 6-3. The discussions should exhibit an understanding of the cost (logical complexity) of decoders, encoders, flip-flops, registers, and memory components. Reasoning, not a "correct" answer should be demonstrated. In fact, while the question asks for a comparison of two microprogrammed control approaches, a hard-wired control might be less expensive for the simple machine of the example.

On cost, whereas the horizontal approach uses larger registers and a larger control store, and requires wider buses, the vertical approach needs decoders for more fields. On performance, the issue is whether the decoders will slow down operations with a simple computer.

The decoders for the vertical microcode approach are:

Decoding is incorporated in the ALU of Fig. 6-22, and no further decoding of AF is required.

The shifter probably needs four individual input lines for left, right, straight-through, and inhibit. A 2-in, 4-out decoder (see the right side of Fig. 3-16) will be needed. The signal inputs for circular/not and logical/arithmetic shifts would not be encoded further.

Selection of source and destination registers (SA, SB, DR) would each be encoded and require a 3-in, 8-out decoder.

NEXT is an address that will be decoded by the control store addressing logic and a separate decoder is not required. M and R are lines to single flip-flops.

Problem 6-4. Students should use Fig. 6-18 and define how the features can be used with a fairly detailed example (perhaps an assembly-language program).

Problem 6-5. It is reasonable to assume that load and store instructions take an additional clock time. Decode and source selection, and execution and register transfer each take a clock time. No bubbles will develop on successive register-to-register operations if registers can be selected for a successive operation while being loaded. The resulting codes are:

a. with bubbles

```
        LOAD R[A] R[1]
        LOAD R[B] R[2]
        NOOP
        SUB  R[1] R[2] R[3]
        STO  R[3] R[C]
        ADD  R[2] R[3] R[1]
        STO  R[1] R[A]
        JGT  R[3] #0   L1
        NOOP
        NOOP
        ADD  R[1] #1   R[2]
        STO  R[2] R[B]
        JMP  L2
        NOOP
        NOOP
L1:     STO  R[3] R[B]
L2:          ---
```

b. compacted

```
        LOAD R[A] R[1]
        LOAD R[B] R[2]
        NOOP
        SUB  R[1] R[2] R[3]
        STO  R[3] R[C]
*       JGT  R[3] #0   L1
        ADD  R[2] R[3] R[1]
        STO  R[1] R[A]
*       JMP  L2
        ADD  R[1] #1   R[2]
        STO  R[2] R[B]
L1:     STO  R[3] R[B]
L2:          ---

* moved to remove bubble
```

17

Problem 6-6. Students might refer to a text on computer logic design or on computer algorithms. We are not designing a hardware multiplier and are constrained to use the registers available in the simple computer. There are many algorithms for multiplication of sign-magnitude, 1's-complement, and 2's-complement numbers. I like the one for 2's complement fractional binary values that follows. It is expressed using ISP (LSR means logical shift right). We place the multiplier in R0, the multiplicand in R2, a shift count (one less than the number of bits in a word) in R3. The double-precision result ends in R1-R2.

        (R0 <- multiplier, R1 <- 0000h, R2 <- multiplicand,
         R3 <- 000Fh); {initial values in registers}
        R2<15> EQ 1 -> (R0 <- NOT R0 + 1, R2 <- NOT R2 + 1);
         {2's complement both to set multiplicand positive}
        WHILE R3 GT 0000h -> (R2<0> EQ 1 -> R1 <- R1 + R0 {add
        multiplier value}; LSR (R1 @ R2) {shift both right};
        R1<15> <- N {fill sign bit}; R3 <- R3 - 1);

The result is a 32-bit 2's-complement value (binary point after the msb of R1) with a lsb of 0. For storing in Mp, the word in R2 would be shifted right and the sign bit copied from the first to the second word, or the bit would be filled with zero.

Problem 6-7. Students can interpret condition "a" as each instruction must start on a word boundary, or no instruction can cross a word boundary. I'll call the former a':

Code in memory, two instructions/word (addr means address of):

```
           a                        a'                        b
LOAD R0      addr A      LOAD R0        addr A      LOAD R0        addr A
LOAD R1      addr B      LOAD R1        addr B      LOAD R1        addr B
ADD  R0      addr C      ADD  R0        addr C      ADD  R0        addr C
COPY R1 R2 NOOP          COPY R1 R2 NOOP            COPY R1 R2 SUB   R2
SUB  R2      addr D      SUB  R2     addr D         addr D         MUL  R0 R2
MUL  R0 R2 SUB  R0 R1    MUL  R0 R2 NOOP            SUB  R0 R1 STOR R1
STOR R1      addr X      SUB  R0 R1 NOOP            addr X         DIV  R2 R0
DIV  R2 R0 NOOP          STOR R1        addr X      STO  R2        addr Y
STO  R2      addr Y      DIV  R2 R0 NOOP
                         STO  R2        addr Y
```

```
Timing:     1   2   3   4   5   6   7   8   9  10  11  12  13  14  15  16  17  18

a  Memory  w0  w1  w2  rA  rB  rC  w3  w4  w5  rD  w6  w7  w8  sX              sY
   Ins.Dec.     i0  i1  i2              i3  i4  i5  i6  i7  i8  i9
   Ins.Ex.      i0  i1  i2              i3  i4  i5  i6  i7  i8-i8 i9

a' Memory  w0  w1  w2  rA  rB  rC  w3  w4  w5  w6  rD  w7  w8  w9  sX          sY
   Ins.Dec.     i0  i1  i2              i3  i4  i5  i6      i7  i8  i9
   Ins.Ex.      i0  i1  i2              i3  i4  i5  i6      i7  i8-i8 i9

b  Memory  w0  w1  w2  rA  rB  rC  w3      w4  w5  rD  w6  w7  sX              sY
   Ins.Dec.     i0  i1  i2              i3  i4  i5  i6  i7  i8  i9
   Ins.Ex.      i0  i1  i2              i3  i4  i5  i6  i7  i8-i8 i9
```

In the timing charts, w means word, r means read data, s means store data, i means instruction.

Problem 6-8. Instructions W, X, Y, Z . . . can be initiated in
2, 3, 2, 3 . . . timing:

```
Clock:     1  2  3  4  5  6  7  8  9 10 11 12
Stage 4:            W     X        Y     Z
Stage 3:         W  W  X  X        Y  Y  Z  Z
Stage 2:      W     X           Y     Z
Stage 1:  W     X     W  Y  X  Z        Y     Z
```

Problem 6-9. Rearranging, to pair concurrent operations, we get:
```
          (A * B) * (C * F) * (D + E) * (G + H)
Step 1:   (T1  *  T2)   *   (T3   *   T4)
Step 2:      (T1        *        T3)
Step 3:                 T1
```

The computation uses four D units (if specialized, 2 adder, 2
multiplier) and four temporary registers (total of 12).

Problem 6-10 (a). The assumptions students make about "charging"
for control in an "ideal" computing engine makes for interesting
discussion. One approach is to treat control as overhead. Some
may include control, converting the program to a sequential form
with goto, and counting each transfer as a clock time. Without
the control overhead the ideal PASCAL program time is:
T_i = t(:=) + (2N + 1) * t(if) + N * t(+) + N/2 * t(:=) + t(write)
If all the t(operation) are unity the result is 38 clock times.

Real computer times:						(b)	(c)	(d)
Program:	00		LOAD	#0		1	3	1
	01		STO	TEMP		2	5	4
	02		LOAD	#18		1	3	1
	03	LOOP:	STO	OFFSET	11 *	2	5	4
	04		SUB	#27	11 *	1	3	1
	05		JGT	END	11 *	4	4	4
	06		LOAD	TEMP	10 *	2	5	h 1
	07		SUB i	OFFSET	10 *	4	3	h 3
	08		JGE	SKIP	10 *	4	4	4
	09		LOAD i	OFFSET	5 *	4	5	h 3
	10		STO	TEMP	5 *	2	5	4
	11	SKIP:	LOAD	OFFSET	10 *	2	5	h 1
	12		ADD	#1	10 *	1	3	1
	13		JMP	LOOP	10 *	2	4	4
	14	END:	PRNT	TEMP		1	3	1
	15		HALT			1	3	1
				totals		263	439	282

Notes: I assume a larger value is found on half the iterations
through the loop. The h in case c means cache hit. The slowdown
of write instructions overcomes the benefits of the cache.

Projects A and B. You should determine how much detail you want
the students to go into in their control description or design.
Please see my earlier suggestions on how to cover this chapter.

Project C. This can be particularly useful if you do not ask for
detail on controls in the semester projects A and B. The results
of this assignment can be compared and discussed in class.

Chapter 7 INPUT/OUTPUT AND OTHER PROCESSORS

This chapter should show the importance of an understanding of
input/output characteristics in computer system design. The
input/output subsystem is the connection between the computer and
its environment. It is too easy to focus attention on the
processor and the memory, since these often are considered the
interesting parts of a computer system.

Students must understand the capabilities of the devices that
represent the external world. This leads to a specification of
the controllers that are needed to connect the devices to the
computer. The connections include the data transfer mechanism and
the controls.

At the interface with the computer, secondary memory units are
like input/output devices, using similar controllers and often
being connected to the same buses as the other I/O devices.
Primary memory itself might use a specialized controller to
relieve the central processor of memory management functions.
Often students are familiar with a particular microprocessor DMA
as a piece of hardware, but do not have a real understanding of
the functions that are performed or of the alternative ways of
performing those functions.

Seeing how an I/O processor can perform I/O control functions
demonstrates how computers can be used in control applications.
The dynamics of input-output operations often establish the
dynamics of the computer. Understanding the relative capabilities
of I/O controllers and I/O processors can be a start toward study
of special-purpose computers.

The special-purpose processors for specialized I/O, for memory
management, for floating-point arithmetic units, and for vector
processing are examples of where the special-purpose approach can
have superiority over general-purpose designs.

Problems 7-1 and 7-2. These are problems that have an indefinite
number of correct solutions. Look for an understanding of the
characteristics and operation of the devices to be controlled.
Have the students considered the nature of the signals, the
number of lines needed at the interfaces, the data rates, the
control signals needed, and the status data available?

Problem 7-3. Look for the rationale used in developing the
"design". It should include specification of the data rates on
the primary memory side of the concentrator. The average data
rate will be approximately 50 term. x 900 mssg./hr./term. x 40
words/mssg. x 10 bytes/word / 3600 s./hr. x 1.2 (to allow for a
header and synchronization) = 6000 bytes/s.. The peak rate will
be about double that or 12000 bytes/s.

The peak data rate on the transducer side is 40 wd./s x 10
bytes/wd. x 1.2 = 480 bytes/s. for each transducer. The average
is about 120 bytes/s. per transducer. The overall data rate of
12000 bytes/s. allows for 25 terminals operating at peak rate.

Buffering will be required to allow for simultaneous transmission
by several terminals. If half the terminals send messages in a 20

20

second time period, buffering of 25 messages is needed. Thus we need a buffer of 40 wd. x 10 bytes/wd. x 1.2 x 25 = 12000 bytes. It is feasible to provide at least 32000 bytes in such a buffer.

Students' designs should show LRC, parity checking, and adding an identifier at each input line from terminals. There should be a message concentrator function, a message buffer, and controls. Many students will provide acknowledgement of receipt of terminal messages by the computer. Many of the queuing techniques discussed in Chapter 9 are applicable, but most students will not be familiar with those techniques at this point.

Problem 7-4. Answers should demonstrate an understanding of the two approaches to input/output addressing. Memory-mapped I/O simplifies the instruction set, since I/O commands are simple MOVE instructions involving data in memory. On the other hand, memory-mapped I/O can interfere with other memory operations if there is a large amount of I/O traffic. In the latter case a separate buffer and independent I/O control might be superior. This is a step toward introduction of an I/O processor.

Problem 7-5. When DMA is used with a modular system with multiple Mp, Pc, and Kio (or Pio) modules, the DMA must determine which Mp is being addressed by which Kio. It must inhibit all Pc from attempting to gain access to that Mp module, but should permit each Pc to address other Mp modules. The problems are related to communication among modules and control of memory addressing by Pc units. This is a good problem for classroom discussion.

The DMA function units can be associated with Pc, Mp, or Kio modules. In each case the Pc will be inhibited from transmitting memory commands to the selected Mp address range and will signal the DMA that it can permit the Kio to address Mp. When the I/O transaction is complete, the DMA must release the Pc to address that range of Mp. Additional DMA/Pc and DMA/Kio communication (transfer complete) is required beyond that of Fig. 7-11.

If the DMA is associated with Pc modules, the DMA REQ signal will be broadcast from the initiating Kio to all DMA units. The Kio must receive the ACK signal from all DMA before it initiates a memory transfer. When the transfer is complete the transfer complete signal is broadcast to all DMA units. The connections between a DMA and its Pc are similar to those of Fig. 7-11, except that a release signal must be transmitted.

When the DMA is at a Mp module, the Kio sends a DMA REQ to the DMA for Mp being addressed, and will receive the ACK from that DMA. The DMA will broadcast to all Pc modules the identity of the Mp module (by address range) that is being requested. The DMA must receive a signal from each Pc before it permits the I/O transfer, and must tell each Pc than the Mp module is available at completion.

If DMA units are associated with individual Kio modules, control of the Pc modules is handled in a similar manner, but each DMA must be able to distinguish which Mp module it wishes to inhibit access to.

Problem 7-6. Students should deduce how a bus is controlled and how arbitration of bus conflicts is achieved. They should note which input signals are common to both units, are complementary, and are outputs from the other unit. They should not be expected to have precise descriptions. Text reference [Intel83] describes the signals as follows (most Multibus signals are in Fig. 7-17):

Common or complementary signals:
        S_0, S_1, S_2, Processor status.
        CLK, Clock, from 8284 Clock Generator.
        IOB, IOB', I/O bus mode.
        AEN, Address enable.

8288-unique signals:
        CEN, Command enable.
        MRDC, MWTC, Memory read and write commands.
        IORC, IOWC, I/O read and write commands.
        AMWC, AIOWC, Advanced memory and I/O write commands.
        INTA, Interrupt acknowledge.
        DT/R, Data transmit/receive.
        DEN, Data enable.
        MCE, Master cascade enable (dual-function pin).
        PDEN, Peripheral data enable (dual-function pin).
        ALE, Address latch enable.

8289-unique signals:
        LOCK, Lock control.
        CRQLCK, Common-request lock control.
        RESB, Resident bus option enabled.
        ANYRQST, Request priority-setting mode control.
        SYSB, System bus request (if RESB is off).
        INIT, Initialize system.
        BCLK, Bus clock.
        BREQ, Bus request.
        BPRI, BPRO, Bus priority in and bus priority out.
        BUSY, Bus busy.
        CBRQ, Common bus request.

Problem 7-7. Figure 7-26 shows more detail of the computer interface control signals (left side) than does Fig. 7-27 (right side). Ten individual signal lines of the former perform the function described as "Bus Arbitration" in the latter. At the network interface, Control Status of Fig. 7-27 covers signals similar to TxRDY (transmitter ready), TxE (transmitter empty), RxRDY (receiver ready), and SYNDET/BRKDET (synch or break detect). The signals TxC (transmitter clock), TxD (transmitted data), RxC (receiver clock), RxD (received data) of Fig. 7-26 have similarly named signals in Fig. 7-27.

The Intel Data bus buffer performs the same functions as the National I-O buffers. Read-write control logic of the 8251A is like DMA buffer-control logic of the NS32490. Modem control is not included in Fig. 7-27. The NS32490 Transmit/receive FIFO serves as both Transmit buffer and Receive buffer. The separate Transmit and Receive control functions of the 8251A are performed by the following in the NS32490: CRC generator/checker, Transmit serializer, Receive deserializer, Preamble/synch, Receive byte count/alignment, Address registers, Address recognition, Protocol PLA, and Collision recovery.

The 8251A is simpler, whereas the NS32490 is more flexible (more a general-purpose controller).

Problem 7-8. This problem can lead to interesting discussion in class. National placed the following instructions in the central processors (NS32032 and NS32016) to handle MMU operations:

LMR, load MMU register.
SMR, store MMU register.
RDVAL, validate read address.
WRVAL, validate write address.
MVSU, move from system to user space.
MVUS, move from user to system space.
BPT, breakpoint trap (see Fig. 6-18).

Problem 7-9. Some of the information flow can be deduced from the text and from Fig. 7-30. Students must "invent" aspects of the flow that are not described or shown. Students should describe the flow of instructions and data from/to I/O devices, loading of registers from table memory, operations on the data and on addresses by the 3 ALUs, and return of results to registers in table memory.

The large (1024 word) instruction cache allows instructions for large loops to be held in the processor, leading to effective vector processing. The subroutine stack holds pointers for storing and recovery of environments. Concurrency is effected by performing address calculations in the address unit while previous instructions are executed (possibly concurrently) in the adder and multiplier units. Registers hold 64 data words and 64 argument addresses. The large number of registers and the independent adder and multiplier units are very effective for combined multiply-and-add operations that are so common in matrix algebra.

Problem 7-10. Discussion should focus on the large number of registers (16 banks of 32 to 256 registers each) to hold vector data. The processor can use register-to-register operations, requiring very few Mp references. VMR, VSR, and VAC allow for control of repeated operation sequences that are characteristic of vector processing. The instructions that were added to the System/370 instruction set (see p. 294) facilitate vector manipulation in conjunction with the added registers.

Projects 7-A and 7-B. The assignments for this phase of the continuing projects are straightforward steps in the project assignments.

Project 7-C. This assignment can call for a very detailed design or just an overview, depending on the students' backgrounds.

Chapter 8 PARALLEL COMPUTER SYSTEMS

This chapter presents an overview of parallel computation, a topic that can be the subject of a whole course for graduate study. The chapter starts with a review of the need for concurrent processing, defines some classes of processors, and presents some background on high-performance computers.

Vector and array processing, and processors designed specifically for their accomplishment, are major subjects in studying parallel processing and of supercomputers. There is opportunity to assign interesting reading from contemporary technical literature to supplement the text, if you so desire. The topics can be covered in great detail if there is time. Section 8.6 extends the discussion to even more flexible (and potentially powerful) MIMD computers.

If you plan to cover parallel processing in more than a cursory way, Section 8.5 on interconnection is important, since communication among the many modules of a parallel system often forms the bottleneck that limits performance. Performance of parallel systems of both SIMD and MIMD types is covered by reviewing some principles and by outlining studies of the topic. Again, there is opportunity for outside reading and there will be many interesting papers that postdate the text on the topic.

Problem 8-1 (a). Conflicts can occur for several reasons. For example, instructions G[1] <- G[3], G[0] <- G[2] both require the MOVE unit and cannot be executed concurrently. The instructions G[1] <- G[3], G[1] <- G[0] + G[2] share a common destination register and are in conflict. In each case one instruction should be delayed until the other has been executed. The instructions G[1] <- G[3]; G[2] <- G[0] + G[1] cannot be executed concurrently since the second requires the result of the first. The CDC 6600 and several successors in the Cyber family have more independent function units, and can have conflicts from more complicated instruction combinations.

(b). An ISP for the conflict resolver, like the CDC scoreboard, must include busy bits for the two function units and reserved bits for destination registers. The two function units need registers to hold the operator codes and the source and destination register designators. Instruction execution in the concurrently operating function units will include a mechanism to resolve conflicts by testing and setting busy bits and reserved bits. Source and destination register designations of each instruction must be tested against the destination register of the previous instruction. Comparing and discussing students' results in class can be interesting.

Problem 8-2. The issues here are larger scale extensions of those covered in Problem 8-1. The key question is, "Are the program segments and data items truly independent?" Program segments are independent unless explicitly connected by control actions or implicitly connected by shared data. Connection through control actions is handled by the operating system, using some mechanism like semaphores (see any text on multiprocessing operating systems) for synchronization. Data items can be analyzed by the programmer to determine how they are shared (are non-independent)

24

in sequence by different program segments, or are operated on concurrently by the same program segment.

Data dependencies can be identified by a programmer, or by a compiler, to determine where in a program communication and synchronization among concurrently active program segments are needed. A general principle employed in multiprocessing operating systems is that commands, including large program segments, that can be executed sequentially in arbitrary order and produce a correct result can be executed concurrently on a multiprocessor or multicomputer system.

Problem 8-3. The pipeline function unit of Fig. 6-25(b) is defined in the example on page 232 as a dynamic multifunction unit. As such, multiple different operations can be active in the pipeline at one time. The conflicts of multiple sequential functions described on page 232 must be considered. If the multifunction pipeline was static only one function could be performed at one time, but multiple data items using the function could be in process in the pipeline at one time. This simpler pipeline could be useful in vector operations. The dynamic pipeline is more useful for SISD processing, where it is unlikely that a function can be repeated many times. The complexity of the dynamic pipeline results from the control needed for changing the connections among function units. Students should understand operation of each type of pipeline and, perhaps with an example, should demonstrate the differences in operation of the two.

Problem 8-4 (a). The problem is that the calculation for each I is dependent on A[I], and will have different delays, dependent on A[I] for the previous value of I. If there is a separate division unit, successive instructions will be directed to a function unit dependent on the value of A[I]. Students should identify the type of pipeline and show the control to effect the proper delay, and the means to be used to ensure that each of the calculated A[I] is associated with the proper I.

(b). In this case all N + 1 - I should be calculated and The values A[N + 1 - I] obtained from memory as a part of the stream of pipelined instructions. The assignment is effected only for those cases where the unchanged A[I] > 1. This is straightforward pipeline operation. The issues of concurrency have to do with whether the assignment affects the value of A[I] for the test A[I] > 1. Unless we define the concurrent operation as causing the test of all A[I] to be performed before any assignment, the concurrent statement will be indeterminate.

Problem 8-5. For any value of I, A[I,1], A[I,2], A[I,3] and A[I,4] must be in different modules. For any value of J, A[1,J], A[2,J], A[3,J], and A[4,J], must be in different modules. The assignment of A[I,J] to memory can be effected as: location (in module) := I - 1, module := (J + I - 2)MOD 4. The result is:

Module		0	1	2	3
Location	0	A[1,1]	A[1,2]	A[1,3]	A[1,4]
	1	A[2,4]	A[2,1]	A[2,2]	A[2,3]
	2	A[3,3]	A[3,4]	A[3,1]	A[3,2]
	3	A[4,2]	A[4,3]	A[4,4]	A[4,1]

<u>Problem 8-6</u>. This problem is not difficult, but it demonstrates to students how the routers and the networks operate. Any of the 3-stage 8 x 8 networks can be extended to a 64 x 64 network by placing 16 of them in an array N[i,j] where (i = 0..7, j = 0,1). This makes the network a 6-stage 64 x 64 network. The k = 0..7 output connections from each N[i,0] network are to the k input of the N[(i + k)MOD 8, 1] network. Broadcasting with the 2-function router switches will require 64 transmission cycles, since an input is connected to only one output at a time. If each router had a message buffer, the broadcasting could be done in 12 steps (2 at each stage). With the omega network (and the other two, if 4-function routers were used), since any router input can be connected to both outputs, the 2 outputs of a router go to different routers at the next stage, and any network input can be directed to any network output, the broadcasting can be accomplished with a single message transmission, once the router connections have been set.

<u>Problem 8-7</u>. Students can develop the solution by using examples or by employing algebra. Adjacent elements of rows are stored in adjacent modules, the distance between the elements (the stride) is 1. There is no memory access conflict in retrieving a row as long as $p > n + 1$. The stride for a column is $n + 1$ and adjacent elements are stored in modules $s, s + i * (s + 1)$ MOD $p, \ldots$ ($i = 0..m$). There is no memory access conflict in retrieving a column as long as $p > n + 1$. Similarly, for major diagonals there is no conflict if $p > n + 2$. For minor diagonals $p > n$. If the number of columns is greater than p, there is no conflict to linear subsets of columns if $(n + 1)$ MOD p NE 0 ; of major diagonals if $(n + 2)$ MOD p NE 0; and of minor diagonals if n MOD p NE 0. Any of the inequalities will hold if r MOD p (r = n, n + 1, n + 2) is divided by any integer and p should be a prime number. In order for all three inequalities to hold for many values of n, p should be a relatively large number.

The discussion of the prime memory of the BSP is covered very briefly in the text. The BSP itself used an alignment network that moved the adjacent elements of rows, or columns, or diagonals stored in M memory modules to N processors in an optimum way. This was done by ignoring certain memory locations following the plan: if a is the linear address of an element then the module number k = a MOD M, and the location in the module l = a DIV 6 (DIV is integer divide).

<u>Problem 8-8</u> (a). The timing diagram for the pipelined processor:

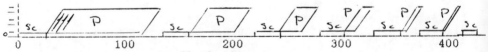

Clock times

Elapsed time, T = 24*6 + 16*7 + 3*(31 + 15 + 7 + 3 + 1) = 427
Processor time, P = 11 x 427 = 4697 (processors x elapsed time)
Scalar processing time, S = 24*6 + 16 = 160
Pipeline   "   " , R = 16*(32 + 16 + 8 + 4 + 2 + 1) = 1008
Total processing time, Q = 1168
Utilization, U = Q / P = 1168 / 4697 = .25

Problem 8-8 (b). For the array processor:

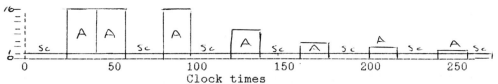

Clock times

Elapsed time, T = 24*6 + 32 + 16*6 = 272
Processor time, P = 17 x 272 = 4624 (processors x elapsed time)
Scalar processing time, S = 24*6 + 16 = 160
Array   "   ", R = 16*(32 + 16 + 8 + 4 + 2 + 1) = 1008
Total processing time, Q = 1168
Utilization, U = Q / P = 1168 / 4624 = .25

Problem 8-9. Hwang and Briggs develop pipelined vector processor
times as follows:
Assume that instruction times and instruction times per stage are
uniform.

$$S_k = T_1 / T_k,$$
   where T_1 is for 1 stage and T_k for k stages.
$$T_1 = T * n * N_{ave},$$
   where T is single instruction time,
   n is number of instructions,
   N_{ave} is average number of vector arguments.
$$T_k = T[n * (k - 1) + n * N_{ave}]/k,$$
   T/k is the instruction execution time per stage;
   it takes (k - 1) times to fill the pipe,
   which is filled n times (once for each vector);
   and $n * N_{ave}$ is n instructions on N_{ave} arguments.
Thus $S_k = (k * N_{ave})/(k - 1 + N_{ave})$.

Problem 8-10. A plot of execution time, T, against number of
processors, N, is:

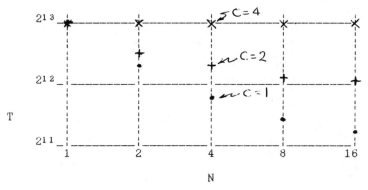

N

Projects 8-A and 8-B call for investigation of parallel-computer
alternatives to the organizations of the computers that were the
subjects of the term projects. Good classroom discussion can
result. If any of the computers designed or evaluated by students
during the course of Projects A or B include parallel features,
these can be compared with the ideas that come from the Project
8-A or 8-B investigations.

Chapter 9 SPECIAL-PURPOSE COMPUTING SYSTEMS

I suggest that you review this chapter carefully to determine the
depth to which you wish to cover the topics, or if you want to
include the material at all. You can merely refer the students to
the chapter for later reading.

In teaching the subject of computer architecture I have found it
useful to develop the progression from special to general-purpose
computers that has been experienced so often. This has been true
particularly in the progression from special-purpose system to
customized supercomputer to high-performance end of a standard
general-purpose product line. Review of the progression helps
students understand computer requirements more clearly.

In the text I review the rationale I have used to approach
special-purpose design in the past and I have extended this
rationale to a number of other examples. Whereas my search-radar
data processor example is over 30 years old, the methodology (and
the architecture itself, albeit with new technology) are still
applicable.

The discussion of alternative approaches to computer control
reflects results of fairly recent research thrusts. While the
extent to which data flow, graph reduction, and systolic arrays
will be used for computer control is speculative, the concepts
stimulate discussion about alternatives to the von Neumann
control structure.

Examples might be the best way to demonstrate features of
special-purpose designs. Accordingly, I have included a number of
examples of special-purpose computers. The examples demonstrate a
variety of applications and approaches to computer organization.
You may wish to introduce other examples from recent articles.

Problem 9-1. This problem involves significant program design and
requires an understanding of the special-purpose data processor
described in the text and of a general-purpose computer ISP. My
example solution uses a hypothetical computer that has features
of many commercial microprocessors. Since all three conventional
microprocessor architectures described in Appendix B (80386,
M68000, NS32032) have eight general registers, I have assumed the
same number in my design.

The program below is for a hypothetical computer that is an
extension of the simple computer of Fig. 6-4. The simple
instruction set allows for one-, two-, or three-byte instructions
with zero or one, two, or three arguments, respectively. Argument
fields in an instruction include a two-bit mode designator and a
three-bit register selector. The modes are register direct
(R[n]), register indirect (iR[n]), register based (bR[n]@m), and
immediate (#m). If an argument is register based, a 16-bit
(two-byte) positive integer follows the instruction. An immediate
nonnegative argument of less than eight can be represented in the
register field of the instruction. Other immediate arguments are
16-bit (two-byte) signed integers following an instruction. An
instruction, then, can be from one to nine bytes long.

A simple instruction set is used. The two-argument instructions include a MOV that allows for load, store, and memory-mapped I/O. The three-address arithmetic operations ADD, SUB, and MUL; logical, arithmetic, and circular shift left or right LSL, LSR, ASL, ASR, CSL, CSR; and unconditional or unconditional jumps JMP, JEQ, JNE, JLT, JLE, JGT, JGE are included. I did not include a floating-point unit, since the real values for PULSE, QUANT, UPPER, and LOWER can be handled by scaling (e.g., PULSE * k > QUANT * k). DET is scaled to m * DET and multiplication by a fractional constant (DETCONST) is accomplished by integer multiplication by n * DETCONST, and a right shift to divide by n (m * DET * n * DETCONST / n). In the example m = n = 64 (2^6).

Effective memory access time (with a cache) is two clock periods. Short register-to-register operations take one clock period, multiply takes two clock periods, and shifts take a clock period per step. Memory references, including offsets for based references and long immediate arguments take two clock periods and mask short-operation times. Jump operations also take two clock periods, since the instruction queue is bypassed.

The example that follows includes the uses of the eight registers and the assembly-language program with its data locations. A simple two-pass replacement algorithm for register assignment minimizes memory references. The message buffers (REPREC) are held in an array, rather than a linked list, and a counter (REPCOUNT) identifies how many buffers are in use. Execution times for each instruction are shown in parentheses, and are followed by a reference to the PASCAL program being executed.

```
Register use:   R[0], 65 ({data base address)
                R[1], MAXRANGE (1500)
                R[2], QUANT * k
                R[3], BOX[I] address
                R[4], I (RANGE)
                R[5], PULSE * k, RL/2, AC, REPORT
                R[6], DET, REPCOUNT
                R[7], TARG, REPORT, REPLIST
```

```
00        MOV #65, R[0]           (2) DATA base address
01        MOV bR[0]@0, R[1]       (4) MAXRANGE
02        MOV bR[0]@2, R[2]       (2) QUANT * k
03        MOV #0, bR[0]@1         (4) initialize AC
04        MOV #0, bR[0]@7         (4)     "       REPCOUNT
05        MOV #0, bR[0]@6         (4)     "       MSSGE
06        MOV #73, r[3]          (2) BOX base address
07        MOV #1, R[4]           (1) for I:= 1
08 L1:    JGT R[4], R[1], L2     (2) I > MAXRANGE
09        MOV #0, bR[3]@0         (4) initialize TARG := false
10        MOV #0, bR[3]@1         (4)     "       DET := 0
11        MOV #0, bR[3]@2         (4)     "       RL := 0
12        ADD R[4], #1, R[4]      (1) increment I
13        ADD R[3], #3, R[3]      (1) next BOX
14        JMP L1                  (2) initialization loop
15 L2:    MOV #73, R[3]          (2) BOX base address
16        MOV #1, R[4]           (1) for I := 1
17 L3:    JGT R[4], R[1], L8     (2) I > MAXRANGE
18        MOV {input}, R[5]      (4) PULSE * k
19        MOV bR[3]@1, R[6]       (4) DET
```

```
20          JLE R[5], R[2], L4         (2) PULSE *k <= QUANT * k
21          ADD R[6], #64 , R[6]        (2) DET := DET + 1 (scaled)
22 L4:      MUL R[6], bR[0]@3, R[6]     (6) DET := DET * n * DETCONST
23          LSR R[6], #6                (6) DET := DET / n
24          MOV R[6], bR[3]@1           (4) store DET
25          MOV bR[3]@0, R[7]           (4) load TARG
26          JEQ R[7], #0, L6            (2) TARG = false
27          JGE R[6], bR[0]@5, L5       (2) DET < LOWER
28          MOV #0, bR[3]@0             (4) TARG := false
29          MOV #4573, R[7]             (2) REPLIST base
30          MOV bR[0]@7, R[6]           (4) REPCOUNT
31          ADD R[6], #1, bR[0]@7       (8) new REPCOUNT
32          ASL R[6], #1, R[6]          (1) old REPCOUNT * 2
33          ADD R[7], R[6], R[7]        (1) REPORT
34          MOV R[4], bR[7]@0           (4) REPORT.RANGE := I
35          LSR bR[3]@2, #1, R[5]       (4) RL/2
36          SUB R[5], bR[0]@1, bR[7]@1  (8) REPORT.AZ := AC - RL/2
37          MOV #1, bR[0]@6             (4) MSSGE := true
38          MOV #0, bR[3]@2             (4) RL := 0
39          JMP L7                      (2)
40 L5:      ADD bR[3]@2, #1, bR[3]@2    (8) RL := RL + 1
41          JMP L7                      (2)
42 L6:      JLE R[6], bR[0]@4, L7       (6) DET > UPPER
43          MOV #1, bR[3]@0             (4) TARG := true
44          ADD bR[3]@2, #1, bR[3]@2    (8) RL := RL + 1
45 L7:      ADD R[4], #1, R[4]          (1) increment I
46          ADD R[3], #3, R[3]          (1) next BOX
47          JMP L3                      (2) detector loop
48 L8:      MOV bR[0]@1, R[5]           (4) AC
49          ADD R[5], #1, R[5]          (1) AC := AC + 1
50          JLT R[5], #3600, L9         (2) AC < 3600
51          MOV #0, R[5]                (1) reset AC
52 L9:      MOV R[5], bR[0]@1           (4) store AC
53          MOV bR[0]@7, R[6]           (4) REPCOUNT
54 L10:     JEQ R[6], #0, L11           (2) empty message buffer
55          MOV #4573, R[7]             (2) REPLIST base
56          SUB #1, R[6], R[6]          (1) decrement REPCOUNT
57          ASL R[6], #1, R[5]          (1) REPCOUNT * 2
58          ADD R[5], R[6], R[5]        (1) REPORT
59          MOV bR[5]@0, {output}       (4) output RANGE
60          MOV bR[5]@1, {output}       (4) output AZ
61          JMP L10                     (2) next message
62 L11:     MOV #0, bR[0]@7             (4) reset REPCOUNT
63          MOV #0, bR[0]@6             (4) MESSAGE := false
64          JMP L2                      (2) next radar pulse
65 DATA 1500 {MAXRANGE}
66 DATA {AC}
67 DATA {QUANT * k}
68 DATA {n * DETCONST}
69 DATA {UPPER}
70 DATA {LOWER}
71 DATA {MSSGE}
72 DATA {REPCOUNT}
73 DATA {BOX[1].TARG}
74 DATA {BOX[1].DET}
75 DATA {BOX[1].RL}
        . . .
4573 DATA {REPREC[1].RANGE}
4574 DATA {REPREC[1].AZ}
        . . .
```

The inner loop takes 101 clock pulses in its maximum path (lines
15 through 37 and 43 through 45). Therefore the required
performance can be achieved with a 20 ns clock period and 40 ns
effective memory cycle time. Even with today's technology a fast
general-purpose computer is needed.

Problem 9-2. PASCAL program using a procedure for correlation:

```
program XXXXX();
   type MARRAY: array[0..M-1] of real; {renumbered W subscripts}
        NARRAY: array[0..N-1] of real; {renumbered W subscripts}
   var I, J, M, N: integer;
       A, B: NARRAY;
       C: MARRAY;
   procedure CORRELATION (var X, Y: NARRAY; var W: MARRAY);
     var I, J: integer;
     begin
       for I := 0 to N-1 do
         begin
           Y[I] := 0;
           for J := 0 to M-1 do Y[I] := Y[I] + W[J] * X[I + J]
         end;
   begin
     {set values of C[J]}
     {read values of A[I]}
     CORRELATION (A, B, C);
     for I := 0 to N-1 do writeln B[I]
   end.
```

With a floating-point unit added to a 32-bit version of the
hypothetical computer of Problem 9-1 above, the correlation
procedure can be expressed in assembly language as follows:

```
00        MOV #0, R[0]                  (1) I
01        MOV #{N}, R[1]                (2) N value (constant)
02        SUB #1, R[1], R[1]            (1) N - 1
03 L1:    JGT R[0], R[1]                (2) I > N - 1
04        MOV #0, R[2]                  (1) Y[I] := 0
05        MOV #0, R[3]                  (1) J
06        MOV #{M}, R[4]                (2) M value (constant)
07        SUB #1, R[4], R[4]            (1) M - 1
08 L2:    JGT R[3], R[4], L3            (2) J > M - 1
09        ADD R[0], R[3], R[5]          (4) temp := I + J
10        ADD R[5], #{base X}, R[5]     (1) X[I + J - 1] address
11        ADD R[3], #{base W}, R[6]     (1) W[J] address
12        FML iR[5], iR[6], R7]         (6) W[J] * X[I + J]
13        FAD R[2], R[7], R[2]          (2) new Y[I]
14        ADD R[3], #1, R[3]            (1) increment J
15        JMP L2                        (2) next J
16 L3:    ADD R[0], #{base Y}, R[5]     (2) Y[I] address
17        MOV R[2], iR[5]               (2) store Y[I]
18        ADD R[0], #1, R[0]            (1) increment I
19        JMP L1                        (2) next I
20 L4:    RSR                           (4) return to caller
```

Register use: R[0] I   R[4] M
                R[1] N   R[5] X address
                R[2] Y[I]   R[6] W address
                R[3] J   R[7] W * X

31

Inner loop (instructions 08 to 15) takes 19 clock periods (CP).
Outer loop (instructions 03 to 19) takes 14 + m * 19 CP. The
procedure takes 8 + n * (14 + m * 19) CP. If m = n = 100, almost
200,000 CP are required. This must be accomplished in 10^{-3} s, and
the clock period must be about 5 ns, a 200 MHz clock rate. The
effective memory access time must be 10 ns.

Problem 9-3. This problem gives students the opportunity to
review matrix algebra. Gaussian elimination entails solving a
system of m equations with m unknowns by reducing an m x (m + 1)
rectangular matrix to a quasitriangular matrix. In the problem
m = 4, and we wish to solve $|a_{ij} * x_j| = |c_i|$, [i, j = (1..4)].
The algorithm is as follows:
    step 1. Let k = 1. With j = k, find the largest value of
a_{ij}. Exchange the row for that value of i with row 1.
    step 2. For i = k..m, for j = (k + 1)..m, divide each a_{ij}
and c_i by a_{ik} to form new coefficients a'_{ij}, c'_i; a_{ik} = unity.
    step 3. For i = (k + 1)..m, substitute row i = row 1 - row i
to get a'_{ij} = a'_{ij} - a'_{1j}, c'_i = c'_i - a'_{ij}, [i = (k + 1)..m, j =
k..m]. Then a'_{ik} = 0 [i = (k + 1)..m].
    step 4. Repeat steps 1 through 3 for k = 2..(m - 1), forming
new coefficients a''_{ij} and c''_i, and eliminating a''_{ik}, etc.
    step 5. x_m = c''''_m/a''''_{mm}. Substitute for x_m in all rows.
    step 6. x_{m-1} = $(c''''_{m-1} - a''''_{(m-1)m} * c''''_m)/a''''_{(m-1)(m-1)}$.
Substitute for x_{m-1} in all rows. Repeat for x_k, [k = (m - 2)..1].

A data-flow graph for steps 1 through 4 takes the following form:

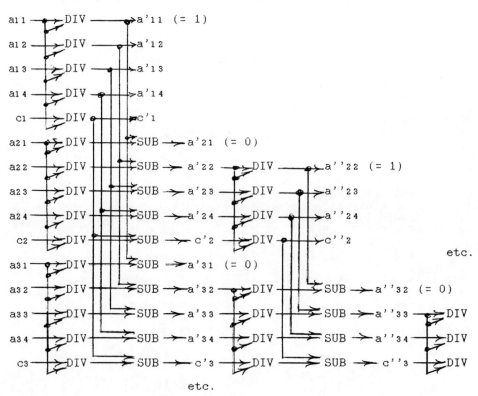

etc.

A graph for the substitution steps is:

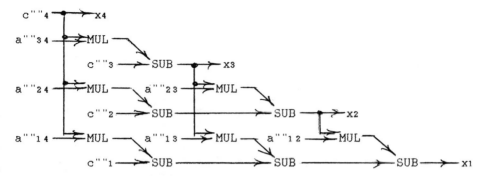

Problem 9-4. The cell functions are:

        Aout = Ain + Bin * C   Aout = Ain
        Bout = Bin   Bout = Bin
        C = constant   C = C + Ain * Bin

With 16-bit processors, the ISPs are:

{Processor State:}   {Processor State:}
    A<15..0>,   A<15..0>,
    B<15..0>,   B<15..0>,
    C<15..0>,   C<15..0>,
    temp<31..0>,   temp<31..0>,
{Systolic pulse operation:}   {Systolic pulse operation:}
    (A <- Ain, B <- Bin);   (A <- Ain, B <- Bin);
    temp <- B * C;   temp <- A * B;
    A <- A + temp<31..16>;   C <- C + temp<31..16>;

In both cases the data format is fractional binary. The
arithmetic function units required are a floating-point adder and
a floating-point multiplier. We could represent the operations in
RTL in four clock times per systolic pulse:

                    t_0 : transfer;
                    t_1 , t_2 : multiply;
                    t_3 : add;

Problem 9-5. Using an example wherein m = 3, large n, and with
the inputs and outputs of cells identified as in Fig. 9-10(a),
the output Y_i generated in each case is shown below. Values at
successive pulse times 1..n are shown as lists. Note that the
first example is useful for continuous streams of x_k inputs,
while the second is useful for fixed n and varying m.

For the left cell (Aout = Ain + Bin * C, Bout = Bin, C = const.):

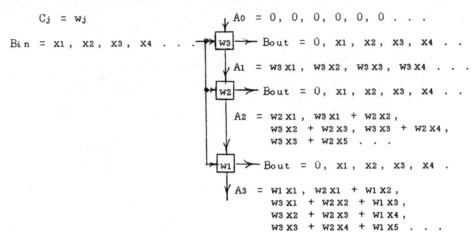

$C_j = w_j$

$A_0 = 0, 0, 0, 0, 0, 0 \ldots$

$B_{in} = x_1, x_2, x_3, x_4 \ldots$

$\boxed{w_3} \rightarrow B_{out} = 0, x_1, x_2, x_3, x_4 \ldots$

$A_1 = w_3 x_1, w_3 x_2, w_3 x_3, w_3 x_4 \ldots$

$\boxed{w_2} \rightarrow B_{out} = 0, x_1, x_2, x_3, x_4 \ldots$

$A_2 = w_2 x_1, w_3 x_1 + w_2 x_2,$
$\quad w_3 x_2 + w_2 x_3, w_3 x_3 + w_2 x_4,$
$\quad w_3 x_3 + w_2 x_5 \ldots$

$\boxed{w_1} \rightarrow B_{out} = 0, x_1, x_2, x_3, x_4 .$

$A_3 = w_1 x_1, w_2 x_1 + w_1 x_2,$
$\quad w_3 x_1 + w_2 x_2 + w_1 x_3,$
$\quad w_3 x_2 + w_2 x_3 + w_1 x_4,$
$\quad w_3 x_3 + w_2 x_4 + w_1 x_5 \ldots$

If $n \geq m$, y_i appears at successive pulses as the output A_3.

For the right cell (Ain = Aout, Bin = Bout, C = C + Ain * Bin):

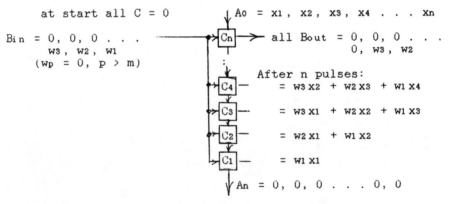

at start all $C = 0$

$A_0 = x_1, x_2, x_3, x_4 \ldots x_n$

$B_{in} = 0, 0, 0 \ldots$
$\quad w_3, w_2, w_1$
$\quad (w_p = 0, p > m)$

$\boxed{C_n} \rightarrow$ all $B_{out} = 0, 0, 0 \ldots$
$\qquad\qquad\qquad 0, w_3, w_2$

After n pulses:

$\boxed{C_4} - \quad = w_3 x_2 + w_2 x_3 + w_1 x_4$

$\boxed{C_3} - \quad = w_3 x_1 + w_2 x_2 + w_1 x_3$

$\boxed{C_2} - \quad = w_2 x_1 + w_1 x_2$

$\boxed{C_1} - \quad = w_1 x_1$

$A_n = 0, 0, 0 \ldots 0, 0$

The correct values appear as C_i after n pulses.

Problem 9-6. In ILLIAC IV a set of D units is selected by an explicit mask in the control unit. Further selection can be accomplished as a result of conditional tests. In PEPE test condition selection also is used, but the initial selection is associative. No fixed selection of a given D unit is established by the control unit.

ILLIAC IV was designed for solution of vector-processing problems in numerical analysis, wherein the pattern is known in advance. PEPE, on the other hand, was designed for association of a radar return to a radar track currently being processed. An associative search was required to find the current track.

Project 9-A. This project is similar to Project 8-C, but is broader in scope. You might find it useful to combine the two projects, using 9-A as an extension of 8-C.

Chapter 10 SUMMARY AND PROGNOSIS

This chapter encourages spirited argument on where the technology
is taking us. If your class includes students with electrophysics
backgrounds they can serve as resource persons to lead discussion
of limits on the trends toward higher and higher component
densities and on alternative approaches to device technology.
Otherwise you might assign a special project to investigate
device technology for such discussion.

It is important not to let a technology focus carry the class too
far from the major topic: the outlook for computer architectures.
Will we see the obsolescence of the von Neumann architecture?
Will we be able to use the capabilities that will be available?
How will software and language translation keep up with the
hardware capabilities?

I have found it useful to cover the material of this chapter at
about the time the students are submitting their term projects.
Prognosis of the future of computer architecture is focused more
clearly when examined against the background of current computer
designs.

APPENDICES

Appendix A: PMS AND ISP DESCRIPTIVE SYSTEMS

In this appendix I have defined the PMS and ISP descriptive
systems in a formal way. While not necessary to comprehension of
PMS and ISP descriptions in the text, the formal definition can
be useful if readers want to describe a computer in significant
detail. It helped me as I prepared the ISP descriptions for
Appendix B, forcing me to be precise in my definitions of the
operation of those machines. Even if you do not assign the study
of Appendix A, I suggest that you point to its existence and its
uses.

Appendix B: SOME EXAMPLES OF INSTRUCTION-SET PROCESSORS

Included in this appendix are fairly detailed (but certainly not
complete) descriptions of several important architectures. The
ISP descriptions are useful for study of the particular computers
and for comparisons of different approaches taken by successful
architects. Students should find that these examples can be
compared with the results of their own term projects. I have
found it useful to compare some specific features of different
architectures, such as data and instruction formats, effective
addressing capabilities, and instruction interpretation.

NOTES

NOTES

NOTES

NOTES

NOTES

NOTES

NOTES

NOTES